Bee-Bop Jive

Only one bee looks the same in these two pictures after an hour of serious bee-bop. Can you find it?

Finish the rest of this butterfly using the first half as a guide.

Butterfly Flutter

Butterfly Doodle

Draw a dotted i.

Add a B and
a curly V...

to make this
butterfly!

Now it's your turn!

Make a Face

Finish these faces to show how each boy or girl is feeling.
Then color their hair and clothes to complete the drawings.

Learn to draw

Use the doodles below to get started.
Finish the doodles by adding details and colors.

OWL

GIRAFFE

Make New Friends!

Doodle features on these faces.

What's the craziest dream you've ever had? When you lie in bed at night, what do you think about? Whatever your dreams are, doodle them here!

Last Night I Dreamt...

Got It Covered

Read the titles of these two books then illustrate what you think the covers should look like.

The Book of My Favorite Things

PACK IT UP!

Doodle what you need for school.

School Bus Doodle

Start with a big loaf of bread.

Add a nose.

Now draw 2 big circles...

and 4 smaller circles.

Add 3 rectangles.

Finish by drawing 2 back tires.

Get on board with your own doodle!

UP AND AWAY

Draw unique colorful patterns on each hot air balloon. The sky's the limit with these doodles!

Bee-Bob Jive

Published by Sequoia Children's Publishing,
a division of Phoenix International Publications, Inc.

8501 West Higgins Road, Suite 790
Chicago, Illinois 60631

59 Gloucester Place
London W1U 8JJ

© 2019 Sequoia Publishing & Media, LLC

www.sequoiakidsbooks.com

10 9 8 7 6 5 4 3 2 1

ISBN 978-1-64269-089-7